Poetically, Therapeutically, Spiritually, Dancing Your Way Out of Despair

Overcoming Trauma

HANNAH OSWINE

WESTBOW
PRESS®
A DIVISION OF THOMAS NELSON
& ZONDERVAN

WestBow Press books may be ordered through booksellers or by contacting:

WestBow Press
A Division of Thomas Nelson & Zondervan
1663 Liberty Drive
Bloomington, IN 47403
www.westbowpress.com
844-714-3454

ISBN: 978-1-6642-0997-8 (sc)
ISBN: 978-1-6642-0996-1 (e)

Library of Congress Control Number: 2020921110

Print information available on the last page.

WestBow Press rev. date: 11/25/2020

Dedication

To Claire and the countless hours and years of talks, laughter, tears, and fun shared.

Your devotion has always been there through the struggles and yes, happy moments too.

Let me tell you something; I love you, my friend!

PREFACE

For by grace you have been saved through faith; and this
is not your own doing, it is the gift of God—not because
of works, lest any man should boast.

-Ephesians 2:8

This book started one summer from collected notes in a journal to release
a mental block from trauma. Months later, I organized it on an antique
typewriter as a journey of self-healing. Several years following, I retyped it
from its original papers onto a computer app. I have read it, and self-edited
the material several times over several years while I was struggling.

I coped and danced, just as the book does, my way out of despair.
The dance I did in my childhood bedroom with dreams at heart and the
songs and poems I wrote then are in this book. The trauma dance I did
as a troubled young girl to release or hide the fear and shame. The joyous
dance came with my baby boy while celebrating motherhood. The hopeful
dance as a woman of faith with a new purpose in life, this dance I continue
to dance.

Are you a river or a lake? Does your life flow with the
choices you make or that naturally occur, or do you stay in
the comfort of the one design that never accepts changes
in life?

A river continues along as a stream, flowing fast or slow,
just as in the movement of life. Sometimes rough currents
in life's travel, but with continuation in the journey.

Flowing with the movement of change. Which turn do I take; what choice do

I make? The adventure awaits with the natural flow of a river.

A lake you enter, a place where there is an edge of containment. The circle of life and its shape is like revisiting familiarity. The comfort of knowing where you are, where you will stay. Calming waters of a lake feel like home. Where peaceful waters flow, and the contentment of never changing. Peacefulness awaits with the still waters of a lake.

The voice of the Lord is upon the waters. Let the waters cleanse your soul.

There are three time periods in my life I separate distinctly: childhood through my first twenty years, darkness the following twenty years, and the light all the years after.

Childhood is a precious time. A time to enjoy life and look at it innocently. We trust our parents to love us, protect us, care for us, and guide us to an emotionally secure upbringing. This bond of the heart carries over to other relationships. How we interact or feel about our families may build or divide our relationships with others we interact with. More important, we trust God to love us, protect us, and be there for us, everlasting.

In my childhood I learned about God in church and Sunday school. And I believed in Him. In my twenties, I tried to hide from God because I lived in so much shame, pain, and fear. In my thirties, I wondered where God was. So much I wanted in life that wasn't happening or just such a struggle to find and keep. In my forties, I cried out to God often. He helped me, healed me, changed me, and strengthened me as I was heard.

Now, in my fifties, I am thankful for the knowledge that God gives me. Knowing He is always there. He finds me, whether I want to be or not. He is faithful and just. He will always be there. God hears me, comforts me, listens, heals, and has constant mercy upon my life. God loves me unconditionally.

Is anything ever really everlasting? We would all like to think that perhaps some way of life is. One's heart may be in search of that everlasting soul in oneself for eternity. A peace and serenity within the heart, mind, body, and soul. True happiness. Growing and changing are the essences of life. Keeping an open mind in new relationships, with new friends, and loved ones. There are times throughout our lives when all this may seem so trying. Yet times when all is worth the while of living the good life God has given each and every one of us, seeing the beauty within us as human beings and the beauty of all surroundings around us clearly.

I think of myself as a river flowing through adventure, rough currents in life, and continuing the journey with each uncertain turn. But I long to be a lake, calm, peaceful, stable. Literally speaking, the dream lake. I want to live on a lake, in a stone cottage, dancing on hardwood floors, surrounded by mountains, and floating on my kayak, appreciating it all.

SEASONS AS NURTURING

The wind blows touches of water across the land. Dry your eyes from the tears that touch a broken heart. Silence in the trees as each blossom may open to the seasons calling.

Winter snows touch the whiteness of a cloud's puff.

Spring colors earth's lawns and its blooms to the fullest.

Summer grows varieties of stems and petals, vases full of joy, love, and smiles.

Fall drops a new change of life as the trees' golden shapes and rustic patterns flow to piles of contentment and solemn sleep.

As helpless as each natural change may God let flow; human hearts and minds can't always find that peaceful change God may intend for each of us. Damaging winds or hail may change the land, just as humans' hands may disrupt all well-being just with forceful, harmful touches. Understanding that the waters change just as a woman changes.

I wrote this poem when I was a teenager, before my body was touched and my soul was in despair.

Soul

Soul of the sea,
Come rushing to me.
Bring not tides of sorrow
But a new day and tomorrow.
Soul of the sun,
Let the day be done.
Yet keep on shining
To brighten those tears and sighing.
Soul of the heart,
Never break apart.
Though loved ones have gone away,
Mend the heart by letting their memories stay.
Soul of the child,
Explore yourself till mild.
Nature at play is beautiful.
All little things are plentiful.
Soul of humankind,
One's life can find.
The reach of a goal
Is in the touch of another's soul.

When I turned twenty, I had to live with the seasons of suffering and despair.

TRAUMA

Rain had come down quite heavily this cold November 2 night. I sat in my first rental home of three months in a town several miles away from my childhood farm as an independent nineteen-year-old. I was waiting for other music enthusiasts to arrive as I wanted to organize a band, with me as the lead singer. Since childhood I have loved to sing, dance, write songs and poems, play piano, and collect music. I dreamed of performing in a band.

When I answered a knock at my front door that night, I found a strange female who was rather intoxicated with alcohol and soaking wet with muddy shoes from the rain. I let her come inside despite her condition. She stumbled into my house. Then I insisted she give me an address to drive her to in her car, and I would take a taxi back to my house. As I closed my door to leave, I noticed the very muddy floor left for me to clean up. I decided to walk to the nearest store to call for a ride after leaving her at the address given. Being raised a farm girl outside a small town, I was not yet accustomed to the city life or people living there. On the farm I lived a sheltered and somewhat naïve lifestyle. I was a big dreamer and had big hopes for my future.

Everything seemed to happen so fast. I hardly had any time to think. A car pulled up close to the sidewalk, and I instantly found myself forcefully pulled in by a strange man and then pushed to sit between him and the male driver. I panicked, screamed, flailed, kicked, and insisted on being let out of the car the whole time. The male passenger pulled out a sharp knife, and I became quiet. It was as though my whole life depended on that shiny object. Shock had overcome me at first sight. I knew I had to keep my sanity and cooperate with these two strangers if I ever wanted to make it home alive. All thoughts matter once you are put in a trying experience like this. All your strength must be used to get free of such a crime and invasion of your safety. I never knew I had such an inner strength until that moment. The strength and desire to live. *Is this the way life will be out on my own, away from the security of my childhood farm?* I wondered. The two men were now laughing at my change in attitude caused by the knife, which was held at my chest in a taunting manner. One asked me, "You're scared, aren't you?" He ran the knife down the material of my pants and asked, "Do you like the feel of my knife? Tell me it feels good." The male passenger tormented me; he found a thrill if my facial expressions showed fear and asked me disgusting sexual questions.

> Fear: Scared of a word, a touch, a sound.
> The faintest breath of my heart pound
> Like a storm in the night,
> When children couldn't sleep without a light.

I was unable to get any passing cars' attention. The knife was near my side at all times and was all that kept me from making any wrong moves. The driver took us farther outside the city limits and my hopes of leaving the car alive dimmed.

> Helpless: No control of me
> Nor daily tasks I try and see.
> A broken wing under the feather
> Stopped the bird's flight in the fierce weather.

Tired, drained, and weary from the several hours of riding in the car with the kidnappers, I tried to keep my spirits up in spite of it all. I did not know how. I do not know where I was. Survival and the will to live were heavy on my heart. What would happen next? Would I ever get to see my family again and tell them that I love them? The car stopped along a muddy country road. The heavy rain was taking its toll on the windshield; it blocked any possible glimpse I could get of escape. The men locked the car doors, and I sensed danger.

> Isolated: Nowhere to go.
> Silence is all I know.
> Trapped like a child's kite

In a tall tree's never-ending flight
Scared: Shaking and trembling so much
By an enemy's unwanted touch.
A baby separated from its mother
Lost security with any other.

I felt numb, as though someone had stepped on me, and I was broken, crushed. I couldn't think, move, speak, or hear anything. I was lifeless. In shock and total despair. I just sat and stared into empty space and empty thoughts. My body was the same—frail, weak, heavy, and exhausted. The two strangers forcefully lifted my body over the front seat of the car. Then they took turns raping me. The knife was positioned as a reminder to do as they said. When I struggled or resisted, they rubbed the knife against my throat.

Shock: Sudden jolt to the mind,
Leaving you cold and blind.
Ice dropped in hot oil
Sends crackled sparks to the boil.
Shame: Embarrassed by the thought,
Perhaps I could have fought.
A runny-nose kid on the stage,
Unable to remember lines rehearsed on the next page.

The Lord's Prayer was now more than ever on my heart; I recited it constantly in my thoughts. Since childhood I have been a believer in God, in a religious perspective. I found myself crying out to Him more than ever during this trauma and in the years to follow. I survived and live only by the grace of God. The years after with post-traumatic stress disorder were unbearable at times. A thousand of feelings came across my mind throughout the months and years that followed.

Everything about myself that I once knew was gone. I no longer recognized myself, no longer had control of my thoughts or actions.

Uncontrolled: Fight back the tears of love
     And even yet, sorrow.
     Truth and strength given from above,
     Yet unable to speak or swallow.
Crying: Tears of pain
     Pour out like rain.
     Tears of fear,
     Hoping someone will hear.

I felt so dirty, filthy. My insides were shaking, and I wanted to be sick. I felt restless and embarrassed. Could I ever trust anyone again? I was obsessed with cleaning my floors. The mud and dirt could not stay in my sight. *Will my floors ever be clean enough again?* The days, months, and years to follow were not the easiest or healthiest. I changed into a totally different person. I changed in some natural ways but also by force as a result of the rape. I felt guilty about the experience. Denial and mental blocks were now parts of my life. Didn't want to accept what had really happened to me.

I felt all the feelings connected with rape but couldn't really see clearly the word and understand its whole meaning. Whenever I heard that word, I would cringe and close my eyes, ears, mind, and thoughts. I would block it out and refuse to listen or understand. Anything to avoid the pain. If I could forget it all, the pain and memories would go away. I was scared of rejection by many other than man himself.

Insecurity: Helpless as one.
     Nature's sky, moon, or sun
     Afraid to be alone.
     Life of hope by the phone.

I felt helpless, as though I couldn't face the day alone, the night's sleep, or any decisions with the sun's rise or fall. I was afraid of rejection and being hurt by words, touch, and even sounds. Afraid to be alone. But no one really understands—even I don't understand—the many negative feelings I couldn't seem to control. How could I express something I did not know or understand myself?

Lonely: Need you tonight,
    Just someone to make it alright.
    As cold as a winter breeze,
    My heart shivers alone at no ease.

I avoided new relationships. The few I had, I wouldn't let them know my wants and needs. I could not trust anymore. This made me angry. I was angry at the thought of my heart feeling this way and angry because two strangers had forcefully put these feelings, and their bodies, on me.

Anger: How dare you hurt me so
    When all I did was say, "No!"
    The roaring sound of hunger
    Over two bears preying for their younger.
Frustration: Can't feel or think today.
    What I said goodbye to yesterday.
    Don't know what dreams are anymore.
    All that's left is a closed heart behind that door.

I became so emotional over the years since the rape. The moods changed so often and quickly. Many days I would just start crying over the amount of them all.

I would feel lifeless and depressed. Tears would just take over my sad heart to relieve the pressure of it all, the pain, darkness, and feeling as though it would never end. A smile didn't exist anymore on this once happy and content young woman. One rude word said to me by anyone would break my heart.

Depression: Sadness sinks in so deep
    One can't think, eat, or sleep.
    Feeling as low as the tide,
    Constant sorrow for loved ones who died.

Depression, a scary place to be. Isolation and loneliness take over you. How did I get in so deep? I am in complete despair. My confidence was no longer there because I no longer knew who I was. Reality was all gone. I felt very unloved. My dreams were gone. My talents subsided. My dancing, my music, all gone. I felt paralyzed by my roller coaster of emotions. I just wanted to scream out the truth of all the pain I felt inside. But instead, I held it all inside me. Felt very confused about everything. Felt like a bird with a broken wing in flight against the wind.

> Confused: Hard to understand feelings.
> Comforting hugs are the only healings.
> Words not making sense
> As I can feel my mind and body get tense.

God, please clear away this confusion that flows into my mind and heart. The flow and sound of rushing, crashing waters over many piled sharp-edged rocks in a riverbed. Carried off to a never-ending sleep, never-ending flow. Everything has changed, and I don't know what to do.

If I could, I would dry my eyes from the tears that pour from my broken heart. Silence with each season changes myself and my life. Sleepless nights and restless days from the nightmares and flashbacks are too much. I am insecure and afraid of the dark. I am living a life in darkness.

As a little girl I was shy and quiet. After the rape, I became a silent woman full of pain, fear, and shame. Fear continued to haunt me throughout many years. I seemed to be afraid of everything. As long as you carry your burdens alone, you don't need a burden bearer. But Lord, I need you!

God bless the women who may not have survived such a violent act as rape. May justice be done for them at peace in their souls by the next woman who chooses to be strong for them both.

I felt your hands today, my Lord and Savior. I lived to tell my story.

FAMILY SUFFERING

When my mother was told about the rape, two shocking statements she made hurt my healing process and our relationship. First she had asked me, "Why did you get in the car?" This set the stage for me to blame myself for the attack for years to come. The second thing she stated to me was that if I were pregnant, I would be having an abortion. It shocked me to hear her say this because we grew up in a religious home. I did not get pregnant after the rape. I strongly believe it was because I was given a morning after pill by the appropriate authorities who examined me for evidence at the police department. But I always feared getting pregnant because I knew the influence my mom had on the choice if I did.

The two men who kidnapped and raped me were caught and arrested. There was a trial and jail sentences. Justice was not served to my satisfaction however. They were sentenced to only two years in prison. More years could have been fought for in court, but my mom told the attorney, without my knowledge, that I was not emotionally up for it. I resented my mom for this outcome and taking that decision of justice from me. I resented the court system for releasing the two men on good behavior before the full sentence time was completed.

My family suffered many losses over a span of five years, my trauma among them. When I was a senior in high school, I suffered a severe head concussion from an incident at a school dance. Mental and spinal complications from the concussion gradually showed up several years after. The same year, a garage fire on our family farm destroyed two cars inside while I was home alone. An electrical spark occurred in the car that I was trying to start so I could drive to school. My father didn't handle the accident well and blamed me, which still causes distress in our relationship. My doctor treated me for shock and prescribed valium.

I have had a sensitive bladder and infections since the rape that continue to this day. My brother's firstborn child dies at the age of four from a rare and fatal bone marrow disease. The following year, my childhood home burned down, and my parents were hospitalized with severe burns and shock. Then my sister's first husband died in a tragic incident, and she later had an emotional breakdown from it all.

> Family: a bond that can never be broken by the heart, everlasting.
> Relationship: a bond given by the heart and must be worked toward the everlasting.
> Friendship: a bond from the heart, giving, everlasting.

I felt Your hands today, my Lord and Savior. And love from Your everlasting relationship.

SIN OF LIFE

During this time in my life, I was struggling greatly with the post-traumatic stress disorder symptoms. My twenties were spent living alone in fear of my environmental surroundings, insomnia, and instability with my work, finances, emotions, and boyfriend at the time. He and I had been dating since high school and before the rape. I valued my virginity and stayed pure the first year of our dating. My first time having sex was with him. We struggled to keep our relationship healthy after my changes following the trauma. He stayed with me for several years, but perhaps more out of sympathy than love and being faithful. To this day I still don't remember how old I was or much detail about my twenties.

Amid all the instability, I found out I was pregnant. Once I knew about the pregnancy, I felt very alone and afraid. There was no one in my life whom I felt I could confide in about this matter. I felt he would not be supportive as we had broken up from our relationship again. I also knew I could not trust telling my mom. My first thought was, *I am not getting an abortion*. I still had religious principles in me.

Distraught about what to do, I avoided telling the former boyfriend for a couple weeks. When I finally found the nerve to do so, he was just as I had expected, untrustworthy. His accusations that I was unprepared to be a responsible mother because I was unable to care for myself were undeniable. Proclamations of his not wanting any part of the situation were utter rejection. With a heart and mind full of great confusion, I found myself in another car, the stranger within myself, and no control over my own life again as he drove me to a clinic. After the abortion, I mentally blocked it out. Shame and guilt was a numbing way to face each day. I shut myself out of my own life, a life of despair.

The decision about an unplanned pregnancy is never an easy one or left without regret, doubt, fear, pain, and judgment. It is a traumatic experience in itself. A decision that I feel needs to be between God and the woman. Abortion is a sin; I will not deny this. My heart was cold, my mind was blank, and my body ached for the little life that would now be a huge, deadened emptiness. My soul was suffering and in despair. I was feeling grief and regret. I hated everything about myself then, especially for what I did. I hated my boyfriend for talking me into this. I hated the men who raped me. I hated my father for always being verbally abusive to me. Truthfully, I hated men. I wanted nothing to do with them.

I never forgave myself. I never spoke of this awful experience to anyone. And I will never understand what made my sick mind so weak to not decide on my own that it was wrong, a sin. I allowed the words from my mom and boyfriend to influence me. I condemned myself knowing I was a mess. The next day, after the abortion, I moved from the rundown house I was renting. I mentally blocked out what happened and never looked back or thought about that painful, regretful experience ever again. My mind and heart felt blank, so I appeared blank. Rejection left me feeling insecure, lonely, and angry. I was filled with shame.

I began to drink alcohol more excessively. I would drink to either remember or forget the previous years of tragedies. I isolated myself and got lost in listening to music at home. I would let myself get so emotionally into the rhythm and the feelings connected to a song that I would cry or scream as a release of energy, and I danced. No one could see, hear, or understand my pain, just as no one could see my passion for music. Both so deep inside my heart, just dying to be set free.

Letting my feelings out was not always so easy as I had kept them to myself for so long.

I was angry at myself and with the men who filled my life with such turmoil. I felt coldhearted, defensive, untrusting, and negative toward others. My few relationships with friends suffered. I spent many lonely nights crying tears of sadness, pain, and fear. I was numb to life. Post-abortion syndrome and post traumatic stress disorder have similar symptoms.

When I started dating again, I was afraid of being touched, afraid of saying no to any man's request or intimate move. I went silent, feeling tense, and I just followed what he desired, whether I felt the same or not.

I believed somewhere, sometime a knife or other method of bodily harm would be there to force a yes. I hated knives and had a fear of looking at them. My thoughts would take me back to the rape every time. I confused love with sex. Mentally I hated sex, and physically, the pain was always there. Broken hearts and false intentions added to this. For many years, bodily touch became the only kind of "love" I shared because of the fear of saying no and the fear of being touched without force at all. It was the only kind of love I knew because I was shown at such an early age. I could not give love other than the kind I needed for myself, a love at heart. I stayed quiet and silent for many years.

It is difficult for women to overcome their pasts unless they confront them. The memories usually resurface, and the truth of this loss can no longer be denied. A life and heart heavy with sin cannot be carried for long. I knew I needed to turn away from sin and back to God. Our sinful decisions in life bear spiritual consequences. The consequences of sin is a dead soul. I actually suffered more because I did not have a committed relationship with Jesus Christ, my Savior. I did not know, accept, or receive His love completely. I believed but did not open my heart to receive. I was hard-hearted. I lived in darkness and lies. Not the truth and light only Jesus can give. I needed to bring forgiveness to my heart so God could heal all the fear and darkness. Fear within, fear removed, with forgiveness. But when, how, Lord?

> Your life was not a choice; it was a gift.
> No matter what size, never give it away.
> All those tears, they are never washed away.
> Pain hidden so deep inside.
> Souls are never free.
> Truth can be revealed in time,
> Heard in a deep word, spoken by a small voice,
> Read in a book believed
> Not by man, flesh of darkness,
> But in the Bible, reveal the light.
> I cared not for you because I loved not me.
> I couldn't love myself because I was broken.
> The heart of love is the greatest.

When you died, part of me died with you.

You get to a certain point in life, especially when in despair, when God starts to make you forget. Forget many things because you had to hold on to all those memories. Remembering everything that happened would be just too much to bear.

> to one a fragrance from death to death, to the other a fragrance from life to life. Who is sufficient for these things? (2 Corinthians 2:16)

I interpret this scripture as follows.

> Death to death: The first "death" refers to sin, living in Satan's strongholds, not in God's commandments or the Holy Spirit. This results in the second "death," as in die, go to hell, no freedom, death.

> Life to life: The first "life" refers to being born again, seeking the Holy Spirit, living in God's commandments, walking in the light, truth, freedom. This results in the "life," as in heaven, life in eternity, God's presence.

I felt your hands today, my Lord and Savior, as I deeply mourn a chosen loss.

NATURE AS NURTURING

I have loved nature and spending time outdoors since I was a child playing around the grove of trees on the farm I grew up on in the Midwest. Imagining my own personal dream house built within the trees, long walks on country roads, flying kites from the open fields, going fishing along the bank of a pond, camping in tents and campers, and loving on the many animals and pets on our farm. I had the appreciated pleasure of attending a small rural school from kindergarten to eighth grade, and then went to high school in town. There are great childhood memories of games played outdoors at recess, field trips to a circus or community fire station, and memorizing parts for the annual Christmas play on the hand-built stage. I spent a lot of time with my best friend, who is still an important part of my life. She and I had fun with long talks and sleepovers. Those times in my life were easy and carefree. When I was a teenager, I saw the mountains for the first time while on a camping vacation in Colorado with my family. A new, bigger perspective on nature was set in my heart, and I promised myself I would return to the mountains someday when older.

I see beauty in God's creation of the land, sky, waters, trees, flowers, mountains, and wildlife. I never stopped looking at nature around me as anything less than beautiful just because I felt lost, ugly, and scorned as a woman.

> Your love tis a rose, which grows and grows,
> A smile emboldened in each fold.
> The gentle petal as your hand to hold.
> Warmth in your heart brought from the sun
> After a tear of rain has begun.
> A rose stays cheerful red when feeling blue

When colored with love by the things you do.
The garden of rose love grows more beautiful
As your love for me continues to be plentiful.

Spending time outdoors in nature and crying out to God for comfort were important in clearing my mind of all the hidden pain, fear, denial, and confusion I lived in for so many years. The unsound nature of all the colors to see, freshness to smell, and shapes to touch were all very therapeutic. I needed a new perspective on my life and a chance to start over again with hope of a better, safer life. So a few short years after the rape, I moved myself and my little dog from my childhood state of farmlands to the mountains out west in Colorado. Just as I promised myself I would when I was thirteen. My dreams to live among the trees in the forest, sky-risen mountains, and interesting wildlife were calling me to make a change. Nature is nurturing. As a young woman, I spent my days experiencing and photographing adventure. I enjoyed long hikes on the mountain trails, jogging up to nine miles a day at times, driving on back roads, exploring the different mountain ranges, fishing on rivers and lakes, camping in tents, staring at the night sky of lights, and snowshoeing the winter depths of snow.

I wanted to see and experience more, immerse myself in the outdoors. So I worked two summers cooking in Alaska at sportfishing lodges. King salmon fishing was an incredible experience. My first summer I pulled in three large salmon in one day, each weighing between thirty and fifty pounds. Alaska was also where I picked up my love for photography. I bought a manual Pentax K1000 camera prior to my first trip there and expanded my hobby of photographing nature, the outdoors. The Alaskan wilderness and midnight sun offered beautiful opportunities to photograph landscapes. I continued to photograph for years after. The adventure opened my mind to the isolation within the vast lands. Isolation opened my thoughts to comfortable, safe surroundings. The wilderness is a natural environment undisturbed by human activity. And this untouched, unknown wilderness welcomed my soul.

I began to remember things from the rape. So I started to keep a journal of all my thoughts, whether painful or confusing. I knew I had to try and remember everything that happened to me the night of the rape almost ten years ago now. It was a long, frustrating process and only bits and pieces were to be remembered. Blocking all memories of everything from the previous years was the only way I knew how to move forward in life. Understanding the connection of silence and solitude of my mind and voice was a survival mode.

And as I journaled my memories and emotions on paper in the quiet lodge cabin during those four months, the flashbacks and mental block began to fade away. The northern lights would appear and inspire my vision of energy and moving forward in life. When I left Alaska that first summer, I had enough information to start this book. Returning home to Colorado and my small cabin there, I spent the winter on an old-fashioned typewriter, typing this book from the journal. My intentions for the book were to help me release the mental block and make some sense of the trauma's aftereffects. Over the following years I sometimes read the papers and reflected on the recovery process.

Alaska and its wild adventurous nature was nurturing, and I returned the following summer. I took a cruise on the Prince William Sound before arriving at the fishing lodge to work. The icy-blue cold waters were filled with whales, seals, and otters. I viewed the glaciers from the front of the boat deck and could feel the cool mist of water from gorgeous waterfalls.

Hearing the loud crackling sound of falling ice sliding off glaciers and hitting the water reminded me of thunderstorms in the Midwest. When I left Alaska the second summer, I flew to Hawaii and enjoyed a couple weeks hiking the Napali Coast, tent camping, attending traditional luaus, indulging in guava fruit, and photographing and exploring the beautiful tropical Island. This was another place I promised myself to return someday. Back home in Colorado, I became involved in a relationship with a man I would marry within a year.

When I turned thirty, having gotten married the year before, I had all the hopes of having children and a home. Unfortunately, seasons of strife and losses ended those hopes.

HEARTACHE OF INFERTILITY

The first few years of our marriage brought great disappointment as we began the long heartache with infertility. I was diagnosed with fallopian tube obstruction, which also left me at high risk for ectopic pregnancies. My fallopian tubes were blocked, twisted, and severely scarred. I had a history of pelvic inflammatory disease since the rape, as an infection occurred shortly afterward and was not treated promptly. Since the rape, I was scared of Pap smears and any medical procedures that involved touching female anatomy. The pain that occurred from the sexual force by the two rapists and the authorities collecting physical evidence mentally scarred me. The pelvic area progressed to excruciating pain each month around ovulation due to the blockage of both ends of the fallopian tubes. During the course of treatment for infertility, I had fallopian tube reconstruction done through laparoscopy surgery. The surgery successfully unblocked and untwisted the fallopian tubes, and so the monthly pelvic pains thankfully stopped. I never did get pregnant, however, as the adhesions remained.

Our marriage suffered eight years with the financial and emotional strain of infertility. Disappointment consumed me. Anger recurred as I was now surrounded by the physical scars from the rape.

God spoke to me during the infertility. He reminded me how much my body had already been through up to my current age of thirty-seven. I had struggled physically with menstrual cycles, the bodily trauma of the rape, pelvic inflammation and recurring infections, uncomfortable Pap smears, false pregnancy tests, infertility testings, bladder sensitivity and infections, monthly ovulation pain, and discomfort with sexual intercourse for years due to many of these medical problems in general.

I had emotional difficulties attached with all these symptoms as well, including the many disappointments. Depression became a challenge for me during infertility. I struggled with weight gain, feeling agitated, and a loss of interest in activities I once enjoyed. Sadness made it difficult to function at work and avoid social get-togethers. God said it was time to let go. Let go of it all, and give it to Him.

I buried my time and thoughts in my first business venture. I owned and operated a bakery and coffee shop in Wyoming, where we now lived. I loved baking many kinds of bread and desserts by scratch. Business gradually grew for the five years I owned it. Then one day my husband suddenly quit his job, which provided a rural home, and decided to move to the Midwest, where his family lived. So we put our belongings in storage and lived in a motel in town until my bakery sold. Several months later, I left the mountain states I adored and an ended business dream to stay committed to a marriage with an uncertain family future.

> And let us not grow weary in well-doing, for in due season we shall reap, if we do not lose heart. So then, as we have opportunity, let us do good to all men, and especially to those who are of the household of faith. (Galatians 6:9–10)

> Trust in the Lord with all your heart, and do not rely on your own insight. In all your ways acknowledge him, and he will make straight your paths. Be not wise in your own eyes; fear the Lord, and turn away from evil. It will be healing to your flesh and refreshment to your bones. (Proverbs 3:5–8)

> I wait for the Lord, my soul waits, and in his word I hope; (Psalms 130:5)

I felt Your hands today, my Lord and Savior, as forgiveness and longing collide within my mothering heart.

THE HEARTWARMING OF ADOPTION

After eight years of disappointments and difficulties with infertility, something had to change. I really just wanted to be a mother. I started to realize that I was focusing more on getting pregnant than I was on the blessing of being a mom. God brought adoption to my heart in so many beautiful ways. I remember one day I was at my work, and a woman came in carrying a newborn baby. As she kindly let me hold the baby, I expressed how beautiful and asked if this was her firstborn. She told me she was not the mother but a foster parent, and this baby is up for adoption. I have held babies before, but at this special moment, my heart was set into the utmost wonderful longing and assurance. I knew right then that my previous years of doubt about bonding with an adopted baby were baseless. I also knew that God had intervened that day and brought forth this baby for a reason. A couple weeks prior to this moment my husband and I had talked about starting adoption procedures. We had counseled with an in-vitro fertilization specialist and came to the acceptance that procedure was not being our best option. I was now sure of the decision to adopt. And I have no doubt that God's hands were upon the whole process.

Approximately one year after the decision, six months in the whole adoption process and six months of waiting, we were called about a baby boy only one day old. What a blessing and gift from God! At the age of thirty-eight, He blessed me with motherhood as we adopted this precious boy. A baby boy was born, the next day a phone call comes in, and by that evening, we are parents! I will never forget the drive to the hospital to meet this precious baby for the first time. I was beyond myself with joyous excitement as I was literally bouncing in the passenger seat of the car, singing repeatedly, "I am a mom! I am a mom!"

Adoption is a wonderful experience and blessing! Adoption is a warm welcome in so many ways for me personally. God answered my prayers to be a mother! He removed all heartaches from the infertility. God's ways are always the most wondrous ways. I love how unanswered prayers still reveal His ways and complete our lives. My son celebrates his birthday every year like tradition. But the day after, he and I have always celebrated The Adoption Day as a family.

> Midnight sun across the sky
> Brings beauty at heart,
> Like a child in a mother's eye.
> Nature's way of an enlightened start.

We are all adopted children of God. Being a mother is one of the greatest gifts God has given us women. I am personally thankful God's plan for my life was to be a mother and adopt a child. My son is a gift, and I know God entrusted this boy to me for a reason. My past painful experiences have all been for a reason too. My hopes were given to the Lord. God has loved me unconditionally and faithfully. I worship Him and give thanks for the precious child He blessed me with. Becoming a new mother myself also helped the relationship with my mother. Feelings changed with a forgiving and understanding heart on my behalf that opened a new closeness with her. The bonding relationships of motherhood are beautiful.

This precious boy and I bonded together at first sight. At first sight! There is a funny but cute story to tell about that. Through the initial adoption process paperwork, the couple has the option of listing preferred characteristics of a child. I marked none, don't care, and no preference to which sex of baby, eye color, and pretty much all on the questionnaire. However, on preference of hair color, I did note I was not too fond of red hair. Well I lovingly smiled when meeting my baby son for the first time as he had the most beautiful strawberry-blonde hair I had ever seen! I held this child and told God, "It just doesn't matter. I will take him!" I experienced love at first sight!

The bonding process for a new mother that happened overnight was the greatest adventure ever for me. I was so happy and loved every minute nurturing and caring for him, reading books while in the rocking chair, laughing and giggling every day, and singing songs and dancing with him in my arms. I wrote, sang, and danced with him his own adoption song. A joyous dance with a heart full of love—and with the best cutest partner ever.

> But when the time had fully come, God sent forth his Son, born of woman, born under the law, to redeem those who were under the law, so that we might receive adoption as sons. And because you are sons, God has sent the Spirit of his Son into our hearts, crying "Ab'ba! Father!" So through God you are no longer a slave but a son, and if a son then an heir. (Galatians 4:4–7)

> Enter his gates with thanksgiving, and his courts with praise! Give thanks to him, bless his name! For the Lord is good; his steadfast love endures forever, and his faithfulness to all generations. (Psalm 100:4–5)

I felt Your hands today, my Lord and Savior. Motherhood reveals grace in life.

ABANDONMENT
AND DIVORCE

The first year after my son arrived was very special as I adjusted to motherhood. However, my husband became restless and persuaded me to help him start a business in spite of my desire to stay a full-time mom. This business was in operation one year and then came the abandonment of everything by my husband. A ten-year marriage and everything we had dreamed of and worked hard for all those years ended from his infidelity. I coped alone with ending the first mortgaged home of only three years, the new business assets taken by bankers, and the hopes of adopting a baby girl someday. And I was now a single mom caring for a two-year-old amid it all.

Bitterness and resentment began to consume my thoughts. The marriage, infertility, and financial and business problems were all hard enough to work through. Stress affects all of us in different ways. Worries and anxiety can weigh you down and affect your relationships. Our marriage suffered greatly from the infertility and financial difficulties; the added stress of new responsibilities he obviously could not endure. Did my husband in hiding really think that I could cope with all the losses and stress by myself?

God did. God heard my prayers and tears and guided me through it all. Just as He had through the other tough times and trauma I experienced in the past. Marriage is a beautiful gift from God. I still believe in it and pray He blesses me with someone else who will never leave and who loves my son and me unconditionally. My parents celebrated their fiftieth wedding anniversary before my mom passed away. My grandparents celebrated their sixty-fifth wedding anniversary before Grandma passed away. Divorce is not something any of us plan or want after our wedding day. But I adjusted and mourned during a crucial time of changes all around me. As the country still mourned brutal attacks and losses, my son and I clung to each other with more uncertainty of the future, alone.

Forgiveness is the only way to heal from this sort of betrayal and helps us move onward in our lives. I have dated very little since the divorce. I have been too busy raising a young man alone versus trying to meet a man. My son fulfills my heart and also the growing need for more of God's presence. God is not just a safe place but also loves me unconditionally, is trustworthy, forever true, faithful, and devoted.

I felt Your hands today, my Lord and Savior, giving me strength to move forward alone.

ABSENCE OF FATHERS

My father and I have never really had a close relationship. During my teenage years, he was harsh on my emotional growth with insensitivity and harsh words. As a developing young woman then, thinking about dating, I needed a morally strong father to influence me in the right direction. My father did not provide this. My father was always so protective of me and didn't show his love in a positive way. The few words he would share were mostly harsh criticism and cruel. This lack of a healthy male in my upbringing added to the conflict of healing after the rape, the divorce, and many relationships.

The weekend my parents had their fiftieth anniversary celebration was the breaking point in our relationship. Until that time I had tolerated his behavior in a fearfully timid way because he was my father. Disapproval of me often set off his temper. During that weekend he had a temper tantrum and rude outburst. He packed my suitcase in the guest bedroom, threw it out on the front lawn, and yelled at me, "I never want to see you again." My son was only age four as he observed this display of cruelty, and he was scared deeply. He has never been close to his grandpa ever since. As a mother, and a single parent at that, I vowed to protect my child. Protect him from the emotional harm that comes with an abusive person. My mom did nothing to protect me from my father and his emotional abuse all those years, and I was not going to tolerate it for my son. Years later, my father was diagnosed with bi-polar disorder. I am thankful he is receiving treatment, and I continue to pray for him. I can love him from a distance and occasionally talk to him on a phone call. I am choosing to remember the good memories in my childhood, when dad took me camping, fishing, and campfire cooking.

My son's adopted father never committed to him and made very little contact the first couple years after the divorce. The few court-arranged weekend visits were either unsafe or unwanted. Disagreements regarding the court visitation arrangements were frustrating and costly. I emotionally struggled with the court system making decisions concerning the well-being of my son. I resented an absent father who expected the child who didn't know him anymore to travel several miles for a visit. When the boy turned six, the father declined to have more visitations and asked to have his rights as a parent relinquished. There has been no contact ever since. I have spent many moments in prayer for my son and his absent father.

Absence of a father, that pain of rejection from someone who is supposed to love you. My son and I have both experienced this pain and loss.

> Father of the fatherless and protector of widows is God in
> his holy habitation. (Psalm 68:5)

When I turned forty, I had just divorced a year before. Now as a single mother, I had new changes in life to cope with. The seasons and river are flowing with the movement of change.

I felt Your hands today, my Lord and Savior. You are faithfully our Father in heaven.

SINGLE MOTHER

Children are gifts from God. And I received this gift with great pleasure. Being a mother is the most meaningful thing in my life! Now as a single mother, I have always made sure that I spend lots of quality time with my son. This is far more valuable to give him than any material possession. The main difficulty, as for most single parents, is financial since there is only one income. I sacrificed my time with relationships to earn that dollar. I won't deny there were several occasions of feeling overwhelmed as a single parent. The abandoned wife, captive by strife, and a little boy's crushed spirit with no daddy in sight. Providing for us on a single income has had its challenges.

After my divorce, I decided I was not going to be on the poverty line for long. I had always been a very adventurous and independent woman. I had owned and operated businesses in the past but either sold or lost them because of my former husband's actions. I had experienced enough years of average-paying jobs and now business losses. I decided I was going to go to college for the first time ever to improve my income opportunities. My interests in photography and the outdoors inspired my career choices. I made the college decision at age thirty-nine, applied, and earned my first grant. I started classes at age forty. The college I enrolled in was two states away, but my son and I both needed a fresh start. So a year after the divorce finalized, I moved myself and my then three-year-old boy to Montana, where I started college. What's interesting is I gained more self-esteem than a better income those following years in college. This was greatly needed after not only the divorce and many losses but also for my whole new outlook on life after the past twenty-five years of constant struggles. My insecurity began to fade away. This reassurance in my heart no one can take away from me. Not even a man can take this away from me.

Being a single mother, not by choice but by another change brought upon me, assured my independent ways have helped me to cope better. I made decisions for myself and my son on a daily basis. I was having a new adventure, this time with a little boy beside me. I taught him how to fish, hike, and camp, and we enjoyed these activities together for many years in the outdoors. Nature continued to nurture.

Friends have been important relationships in my life since childhood. One in particular since we were in grade school is a constant commitment. She is the one person who truly knows me, and I confide in her the most. The friendship dance with her is a strong connection. I have always encouraged my son to make friends and be a good friend as well. Together we depend on friends as our family support. I surrender my independence to God. God is the One my son and I depend on for family, provisions, guidance, and to whom we give thanks.

I am making a difference in someone's life. Adoption is beautiful. Raising a Spirit-filled child is beautiful. Motherhood and being a woman of faith makes a beautiful difference in my life.

Our greatest gains come from our greatest losses. My greatest losses were not bearing babies due to the rape, abortion, and infertility. My adopted son is my greatest gain. Thank You, God, for the gift of children. Thank You for adopting me as your daughter, my son as Your child to the fatherless, and me as his mother.

As a parent it is important to live by example. And when mistakes are made to ask our children for forgiveness. It is good to love and forgive our children when they make mistakes. God's grace in our hearts help us remain in calmness, forgiveness, kindness, love, and no anger. I have not always displayed a good example, but I ask for forgiveness and prayer when I fail. Forgiveness is a gift. We must all learn from our mistakes, not just our children. Adults make mistakes too. Anger and frustration are Satan's work to break up peace in relationships. Satan had worked those quite well in my marriage with strife. Forgive me, Lord, for participating in anger and the destruction of myself and my former husband. I wish I had prayed more for him and our marriage back then.

> Cast all your anxieties on him, for he cares about you. (1 Peter 5:7)

Therefore I tell you, do not be anxious about your life, what you shall eat or what you shall drink, nor about your body, what you shall put on. Is not life more than food, and the body more than clothing? (Matthew 6:25)

I felt Your hands today, my Lord and Savior, helping me plant seeds in raising a fine young man.

DEVOTED MOTHERS

My relationship with my mother was good during most of my childhood. She applied her old-fashioned parenting and was caring and devoted. When I came home from school, she would be there with fresh-baked treats and hugs. My mom loved being a mother, and it showed as her most important value in life. I have thankfully inherited this same quality from my mother.

There were some painful issues in our relationship too. When I became a teenager, she was not very communicative on an intimate level when it came to my growing maturity. My mom preferred to avoid any conversations that pertained to the struggles I endured over the years. She wanted to pretend none of them ever happened. Unfortunately, this trait of denial I also carry on. My mother tolerated my father's behavior and ignored the verbal harshness toward me. I felt very alienated from my parents as I grew older, so I limited the time I spent with them and increased the distance between where we lived.

My parents traveled to Montana for my photography school ceremony. However, one month before my college graduation, my mother passed away from her second battle with breast cancer. When she was first diagnosed, my son had just arrived through adoption. Thankfully, during that time we did not live too far away, so frequent visits could happen. My son gave her a reason to fight the cancer. She loved being a mother and grandmother, and his arrival was long dreamed of by her and I both.

Mom's second fight with cancer was six years later, and we now lived two states apart. I was starting a new life as a single mom and about to finish three years of college. My parents had celebrated their fiftieth wedding anniversary, just six months prior to her passing. Her funeral, sadly, was near Mother's Day. I remember holding a vase of flowers from her funeral on the plane back home to Montana. My heart ached from each question and look, "Did you get those flowers for Mother's Day?" My bittersweet and avoiding reply was, "Unfortunately not." Losing my mom was a big turning point in my life.

My grieving process for the loss of my mother didn't really start until later that summer. For the first time, I found myself without someone or something to occupy my days. My now five-year-old son and I would be apart for several weeks for the first time as he had a court-ordered visitation, unknowingly the final time, with his father out of state. The day after college graduation we moved to a different town and job placement, which left me without nearby friends. Adjustments to my new job in the outdoors were extremely physically demanding. At one point I took a bad fall down the mountain and was injured on the job. Knowing Mom was gone and how much I needed to be motherly nurtured really started to hit me emotionally. I reflected on everything that had happened in my life nonstop the previous twenty-five years, since the age of seventeen. During that summer, I became completely physically and mentally exhausted. I reached a point where I felt I just couldn't move any further, a complete burnout. I had come to the end of myself and knew there was no one and nothing else to turn to. Loneliness consumed me deeply for the first time. So I decided to take some time off from everything—work, schedules, demands, responsibilities.

For the first two weeks I slept and slept and slept. God was really pulling at my heart to allow some rest. I just really needed to breathe and be thankful that God was calling me to be in His presence. My mom was gone. My son needed me. I was a mother. And only God could nurture me like a mother, like a father, and like the great, compassionate Comforter He is.

God graced me with rest, time alone to grieve, to heal, to have new dreams and new challenges. He put new people and opportunities in front of me to make some changes. He gave me hope. He carried me out of my defeated attitudes. Jesus was bringing me out of the darkness and into His light.

> Blessed are those who mourn, for they shall be comforted.
> (Matthew 5:4)

I now felt so passionate about many things in life. Passionate about my health, mental well-being, my son, attention from new people, memories of my mom, and most important, Jesus. I don't ever want to forget the "movement" my heart and life took after my mom died. She left me with such love in my heart. Mom was the one person I know loved me so very much unconditionally. I always felt her love no matter how many miles between us or the differences we had in our relationship. I felt her love stronger than ever when she spoke her final words to me over the phone, "I am so proud of you."

The morning she died, a spiritual connection occurred. As I was slowly waking up in bed, I felt my back arch and arms slightly lift. And at the same time, I was calling out loudly, "Mom!" I sat up in bed, alert now, and began to sob deeply sob. Seconds later, the phone rang, and my brother told me Mom had just passed away. My surprising reply to him was, "I know."

Over the years there were times when I looked in the mirror and could swear I saw my mom in my reflection. I could see her features starting to show in me. I never did before her passing. Sad, but I know I did not appreciate my mom as much as I should have. We take people and things for granted in life, and it is definitely a shame. All those years when my mom was living, I felt like I had an attachment to life, some strongly received love because of her. Felt like I was connected to a string that bonded us together. When she died that string broke, and I started struggling with the feelings of being disconnected from life, a lonely existence, and like I was lost because I had no mother to look to when needed. She was always the woman who kept the family together, somewhat. Now that she was gone, the family drifted apart. The mourning process, I am sure, will in time change for the better. But Mom as the woman behind me, who created me, and the first person in my life to mean something, that connection, her being gone now leaves just me as the woman. I feel a greater responsibility as a mother to my son now. I feel a stronger womanly instinct upon myself. The feelings are a bit scary as well as overwhelmingly lonely to a certain point. I am having to realize all my strengths experienced and gained over the past twenty-five plus years are just now starting to have meaning and great purpose for me.

All those years living miles away from Mom, she worried, wondered, and missed me so much. Perhaps she couldn't really imagine how I lived.

Many experiences she and I talked of, yet many I spared her heart about. Now that I believe she is in heaven, I truly feel my mom is with me daily through a spiritual connection. She knows how I live, how I feel. She does not have to have the pain of worrying anymore. She is with me in a very special way. I like to think that perhaps with all the good changes that started to happen to me, Mom is talking to God about giving her little girl a break, to give her happiness. I look at life differently since feeling my mom's love deeply now. I always knew she loved me, but hearing hard to speak words on her deathbed and the way God worked between the two of us in her final week of life, something special happened. God created something between my mom and I in different ways. Absence not only makes the heart grow fonder, it also makes it wiser, more appreciative, and more aware. These are things we should never take for granted and make use of, but we don't always. Mom left me with things that I pray she knows she can be proud of.

She loved me unconditionally, and she forgave me when I was wrong. Growing pains exist no matter what age we are. We all make mistakes. We all have choices. But what is in your heart is truly what stays with you. The power of love is truly a very beautiful thing!

I told many people after my mom passed that we were all actually blessed for the ability to say goodbye to her. Not many people get to do that with loved ones as death can come unexpectedly. We were all given a gift to say, "Goodbye," "Love you," and send her home to God in peace. I do not take that gift lightly. I am grateful to God for that, as we all should be. Her time with us was a gift, and her time to let her go was also a gift. Life is precious!

I want to honor her and carry on her special ways. I feel it's important to cherish her and take pride in having some of her traits. There is no one who loves you as much as your mother does. I know this now more than ever. I felt it all my years growing up, I felt it miles away, and I honestly felt it deeply engraved in my heart with her final words to me. I cannot carry her memory as a depression. She would want me to be happy.

My mother's favorite Bible scripture:

> The Lord is my shepherd, I shall not want; he makes me lie down in green pastures. He leads me beside still waters; he

restores my soul. He leads me in paths of righteousness for his name's sake. Even though I walk through the valley of the shadow of death, I fear no evil; for thou art with me; thy rod and thy staff, they comfort me. (Psalm 23:1–4)

I felt Your hands today, my Lord and Savior, communicating two mothers' hearts from a distance.

NEW FAMILY TREE

Adopting my son made new family roots for him. Thankfully, he has a mother who is lovingly devoted to him and planting seeds of God's Word in his life. My son was happily adopted but then sadly abandoned within the first two years of his life. Reassuring him he is loved, wanted, valued, and worth everything God has for him has always been a priority to me. I had so many weeds and uprooted my family tree through all the pain and losses. Seems like even more so after my mother passed away. I never felt like a good seed from my own family after my childhood. Becoming a woman during the painful experiences of my youth caused family connections to wilt away. I tried to weed out the bad, transplant new growth, and feel planted with my family, but never did. Our fathers play an important role in the harvest of life. My son and I both have been weeded out from a steady father's harvest. After my mother died, I turned to God more than ever before. I see Him as Father, family, harvest, roots, and even a nurturing mother. My son and I both really needed God more than ever in our lives. It filled our hearts with love, the need to be rooted and grounded within the Holy Spirit. I needed God to help me raise my son, and he needed the Father.

> Women are like God's flowers,
> Growing into a more beautiful living thing each and every day.
> Gentle, yet can break at the utmost harsh touch.
> Watered with the pure drink of love itself,
> Giving and longing to receive as much in return.
> Many emotions a woman feels and expresses.

Many changes we go through, or are put to, at different times in our lives.

Changes that make us stronger, more pure.

More aware of our feelings we may not always feel comfortable with.

Growing is the essence of life.

Beauty is within a woman.

We bloom when we are rooted and grounded by the love of God.

I felt Your hands today, my Lord and Savior, as we walk together in unity.

COMING TO THE LORD

When I was a little girl, I was very shy. As a young woman, I became silent because of the fear and pain kept inside since the rape. I stopped talking. Silence from my mouth became a way to live in denial. Personal silence found a friend in sound. The sound of music playing filled the void and entertained my mind. I listened to music constantly and silenced the world around me. The louder the better to block it all out. During the years of mental block in my twenties, I sometimes danced to the rhythm of a song and released energy and thoughts in the sounds. Music kept my mind occupied and became a hiding place. I imagined myself as one with music, and completely got lost within it. My desire to sing as did in my youth was gone because my voice was gone. But the connection with music came through in dancing.

I had all the important things in life backwards. Looking for love in all the wrong places and the result caused years of pain. My soul was undernourished. I felt weary from all that had happened in the past years. I needed God to heal me and change me. I was dissatisfied with the way I was living. I felt as if something was missing. I felt empty and a lack of purpose in my life.

Over the years I ran to unhealthy sexual relationships with men, excess alcohol to bury sad memories, frequent dissatisfied job changes, overworking for career success, and those empty flesh fulfillments. Looking for love in so many wrong places. I wanted to feel valued and to escape pain. I took self-improvement, self-searching, and self-involvement paths too often. Mine was a discontented life trying to fill the days with frantic activities and bad habits. Overwhelmed with medical complications with the painful bladder and spine. Many years I was caught off guard by the anniversary date of the rape and when the post-traumatic stress symptoms recurred.

God changed me when I sincerely turned to Him. He brought me from years of pain and darkness into total revelation of light. He led me to people also of faith. God wanted me out of the attitudes of lack, struggle, a victim's mentality, and associations with negative people. But He also showed me to seek only Him first, not the flesh fulfillments I had been running to. God showed me He is my provider. I am not abandoned. I can work, but He will provide overall. My desire for spiritual riches outweighs my desire for material wealth. I am rich in God's love. I finally learned the importance of seeking and loving God first and then love yourself and others in a respectful healthy way. I found peace nowhere except in Jesus Christ. The empty substitutes are no longer needed to find purpose in my life.

Making good choices in life are not only vital to feeling happy but more important, a pure soul. Sin can act upon our lives like an infectious disease, a disease that is only cured by repenting our sins and asking God for forgiveness. Forgiveness is a gift, a gift from God. When we forgive someone, even ourselves, an overwhelming comfort of peace and moving forward in life comes upon our hearts. The sooner we accept that gift, the sooner we receive joy. God showed me I needed to forgive so I could let go of the pain and anger. Forgive the men who raped me. Forgive that first boyfriend who persuaded me to get the abortion. Forgive my former husband for betrayal and abandonment. Forgive my dad for emotional abuse. I had to let go of the unforgiveness of abuse, shame, and rejection.

> For if you forgive men their trespasses, your heavenly Father also will forgive you; but if you do not forgive men their trespasses, neither will your Father forgive your trespasses. (Matthew 6:14–15)

When I personally invited Jesus Christ into my life, I longed for peace within from the presence of the Holy Spirit. As we remember who Christ is and what He did and can do, fear is replaced with faith, which brings quietness of spirit. Silence no more. I am now a woman who speaks loudly the truth of what Jesus Christ has and will always do in my life. I know where I came from, and I know who is responsible for me being where I am today: Jesus, my Lord and Savior. I am a woman of strong faith!

God brought it upon my heart to rewrite my original book, which had been put aside for the past twenty years now. The journal to the typewriter that was intended to release mental blocks and give me personal healing. I started editing and retyping into a computer program. The book began to develop into something more. I eliminated the terrifying details of the rape and changed the purpose to glorify God and with the hope of helping other women heal. God gave me a desire to share the book. God's story and mine I pray will someday be heard.

One evening while attending church, I was personally brought to a chapter in the Bible by a speaker who didn't know me or anything about my life. But God spoke through her to me, and as I began reading the first few lines of Isaiah 54, my mouth and heart just dropped. "God showed me my life!" He got my attention! This was a huge, moving point for me. I knew then I never wanted to be a silent woman anymore. I wanted to glorify God and be a bolder witness to the power of His love, grace, and mercy.

And as I have now spoken this, reflect on all the meanings Isaiah 54 gives. Reflect on the love, grace, and mercy He has for all of us.

Pertains to each topic:
Rape

> In righteousness you shall be established; you shall be far from oppression, for you shall not fear; and from terror, for it shall not come near you. If any one stirs up strife, it is not from me; whoever stirs up strife with you shall fall because of you. Behold, I have created the smith who blows the fire of coals, and produces a weapon for its purpose. I have also created the ravager to destroy; no weapon that is fashioned against you shall prosper, and you shall confute every tongue that rises against you in judgment. This is the heritage of the servants of the Lord and their vindication from me, says the Lord. (Isaiah 54:14–17)

Abortion

> Fear not, for you will not be ashamed; be not confounded, for you will not be put to shame; for you will forget the shame of your youth, and the reproach of your widowhood you will remember no more. (Isaiah 54:4)

Infertility and Adoption

> Sing, O barren one, who did not bear; break forth into singing and cry aloud, you who have not been in travail! For the children of the desolate one will be more than the children of her that is married, says the Lord. (Isaiah 54:1)

Divorce

> For your Maker is your husband, the Lord of hosts is his name; and the Holy One of Israel is your Redeemer, the God of the whole earth he is called. For the Lord has called you like a wife forsaken and grieved in spirit, like a wife of youth when she is cast off, says your God. For a brief moment I forsook you, but with great compassion I will gather you. In overflowing wrath for a moment I hid my face from you, but with everlasting love I will have compassion on you, says the Lord, your Redeemer. (Isaiah 54:5–8)

Single Motherhood

> O afflicted one, storm-tossed, and not comforted, behold, I will set your stones in antimony, and lay your foundations with sapphires. I will make your pinnacles of agate, your gates of carbuncles, and all your wall of precious stones. All your sons shall be taught by the Lord, and great shall be the prosperity of your sons. (Isaiah 54:11–13)

COMMITTING TO CHRIST

Since childhood, I have believed in God, talked to God, most certainly cried out to Him in times of need. I went to church, heard great sermons, was christened as a baby, and did the "religion thing." But after I committed my life to Jesus, I learned there is a huge difference between a relationship and religion. A relationship with our heavenly Father is beautiful and loving, and not so much rules and reprimand.

A year after inviting Jesus into my heart, I chose to be fully immersed in water and baptized through the Holy Spirit. Baptism is an important part of new life in Christ. It signifies the burial of your old ways of living. It is a declaration to the enemy, Satan, that you have made a decision to follow Jesus. My relationship with God has grown so deeply, and every day is a new blessing of freedom. Reading the Bible daily has brought great revelation to my life. God's Word speaks truth, clarity, and beauty, and to me, it is like reading romantic poetry to the heart.

After my baptism, I was given a scripture that was to represent my inheritance words. The pastor also said that my past sins and pains were to be put aside and my relationship with God restored in full.

> Therefore, behold, I will allure her, and bring her into the wilderness, and speak tenderly to her. And there I will give her vineyards, and make the Valley of A'chor a door of hope. And there she shall answer as in the days of her youth, as at the time when she came out of the land of Egypt. (Hosea 2:14–15)

After I read the scripture, tears began to pour out of my heart as it gave me great comfort and understanding. I interpreted it to mean God wants to offer me some reward, or pleasure in the speaking of great comfort to my heart. He wants to give me love, joy, peace, kindness, goodness, gentleness, all the fruits of the Spirit in general. He provides great comfort from my pains and forgiveness of my sins, the consequences of problems. The vineyards perhaps do represent the fruit of the Spirit, fruit of the Vine. The fruit from the Vine is supposed to nourish me and give me great comfort. God's words speak tenderly to me, and this is the fruit of hope. The door is my heart, and I am to open it to my Lord and let Him in. The land, or wilderness, are where the fruits of the spirit are plenty and grow abundantly. A place I can return to, where I was a virgin in my youth, untouched and unharmed by man, the rape, the promiscuity, and the divorce. My youth as a young woman, a girl, where I was a free spirit and had trust in my heart not only for God but for my fellow man.

As for the story from the land of Egypt, I can be free of my pain, free from sin with forgiveness because of what Jesus's death on the cross did for all of us. I do not have to hold on to the shame, fear of telling others, or any holdings on my life that the past may cling to. I only have God to answer to, not the world, not the devil. I need to put everything into God's trust, His plan, and His great comfort. There, upon God, I shall answer and let everything go. This gives me back my youth because I can act and look youthful in God's reflection of His loving care.

Hosea chapter 2 describes a divorce caused by infidelity in a marriage and rejection of God's covenants. More sin in their lives followed their decisions. The primary theme of Hosea is that God loves His people and wants them to repent their sins and be loyal to Him as their God.

> See to it that no one makes a prey of you by philosophy and empty deceit, according to human tradition, according to the elemental spirits of the universe, and not according to Christ. (Colossians 2:8)

After reading that scripture from Colossians, I came to believe the world is a big lie, deceitful, non effective. To live in God's plan is truth, light, salvation, peace! I want to listen to God and try to obey Him. Listen to His plans for my life. He indeed desires to help me. I welcome God into my life, my daily walk, my success, love, and future.

Jesus says He is the solution for weariness of soul. God followed me through all my pain all those years. He heard every cry, He felt every drop of my tears, and He collected every tear that flowed with the river. His goodness and mercy are gifts. His forgiveness is beautiful. God follows us; He never leaves. He is patient, persistent, and faithfully present. He can be trusted with one's pain of the heart. Truth and trust were two big issues for me. In God, I received both. In others, there was pain in my past.

On one particular second day of November, I journaled a letter about adoption. Later I realized the date was the same as my traumatic rape over thirty years before. This letter reads as follows.

> I am shown God's love for me through adoption. We are all adopted in the Lord. God's plan for me, and my life is beautifully laid out. He indeed knows what is best. I was meant to be with this little boy of mine. Adoption was in my life's plan from God. He has shown me that and more on this day. My body was not designed to bear a child naturally. My diagnosed spinal, uterine, fallopian tubes, and bladder complications over the years remind me with each painful discomfort. God protected my body from more pain that would come with a natural childbirth by blessing me instead with the gift of adoption. During a chiropractor's description of my spinal layout, structure, and problems, I am told it is a blessing in disguise that I didn't get pregnant and have natural childbirth.

> God protects me and knows what's best, as always. Thank You, Lord, for the gift of adoption! Thank You for this precious son I have received! My life is in Your hands, and I trust You. I used to tell people jokingly, "If I could get paid to be a mom, I'd be the happiest woman ever!" Well I realized I am kind of receiving this pay in special ways. God always provides for my son and me. I have always worked to earn an income and have always tried to better myself and that income over the years. Always wanting to raise and care for my son myself and not have

others or a child-care facility do so. Money always came in from somewhere, somehow as God always intervened. Our basic needs were always met, and my son always had a devoted, loving mother there for him. As a single mom, I have received many monetary gifts of support from different generous resources throughout the years. For example, I remember on our move to Montana, waking up in a motel room, walking to the moving truck to continue our trip, and finding an envelope stuck in the windshield wipers. Inside the envelope was a note and a $100 bill. The handwritten note expressed how they remembered long journeys with children and hoped the money enclosed would help in whatever way. I began to cry with a hand covering mouth in astonishment from this unexpected generous gift. I looked around desperately to find someone to personally thank.

We are blessed, and I pray I can give more back someday.

As for you, you meant evil against me; but God meant it for good, to bring it about that many people should be kept alive, as they are today. So do not fear; I will provide for you and your little ones. Thus he reassured them and comforted them. (Genesis 50:20–21)

For among them are those who make their way into households and capture weak women, burdened with sins and sway by various impulses, who will listen to anybody and can never arrive at a knowledge of the truth. (2 Timothy 3:6-7)

There was a time in my life when I began to have more distinct memories of the abortion. I had mentally blocked it out for many years. I honestly don't remember doing this horrible thing. And if a small piece of memory started to come to my thoughts, I blocked it even deeper. This was guilt, shame, and denial at its utmost traumatic effect, and Satan's strongholds tightly on me. Scenarios in public would trigger the memories and startle the disbelief. All were so confusing and numbing. The triggered nudges of seeing antiabortion signs and protestors on street corners started to affect me differently. One specific scenario was when my young son and I were at a church fundraiser. Walking among the tables of quilts and crafts, a display on one table affected me deeply and almost sent me into full panic. My curious son picked up a plastic replica of an embryo and tiny baby showing the development stages. He held it innocently and tried to get me simply to just look at it. A thousand emotions and images raced through my heart and mind. I desperately ignored the replica and the table, and promptly said to my son, "Let's go," as I walked away and left the building as quickly as I could. I didn't understand what was happening to me, but I knew these avoidances of hidden pain were scaring me and probably my son as well. My brain had been locked in a mental state of despair for so long. After the rape, it took over ten years to remember and to allow healing from this trauma. God's grace and mercy protected my mental state until He knew I could handle it. One trauma at a time, preserving my little strength with His mighty love and power. The brain is a mysterious thing after a trauma. But God and His ways are just as mysterious sometimes. He began to reveal to me when the time was right for me to give it all to Him.

> Commit your ways to the Lord; trust in him, and he will act. He will bring forth your vindication as the light, and your right as the noonday. (Psalm 37:5–6)

> For you know that afterward, when he desired to inherit the blessing, he was rejected, for he found no chance to repent, though he sought it with tears. (Hebrews 12:17)

When we repent our sins but keep sinning, we receive no blessings. All we give are tears of pain while living in darkness with the sin. Accept Christ Jesus in your life. Repent of your sins. Receive His blessings, mercy, and grace. God is love, joy, and peace. His compassion and forgiveness are always present.

I began to really pray about the mental block of both the abortion and the rape and ask God for His help and healing as I tried to release them. I decided to receive spiritual and professional counseling for my post-abortion syndrome. A long, deep, and intense counseling that would physically, mentally, and spiritually drain despair from me and renew my soul to freedom. Confessing the sin of abortion and asking for God to forgive me. Forgiving myself was intense because it took the longest time to reach that vital point. Verbally claiming I was forgiven and that sin was gone was major in the healing process. Knowing and trusting God's work on me through counseling to reach those steps of repentance, non-avoidance of hiding, and His graceful healing were all quite miraculous.

God gave me a vision during prayer at one session. The vision greatly detailed Him wiping away my tears and saying, "Come to Me, My child." And yes, I took this to heart for both myself and the unborn baby. I was encouraged after counseling was complete to write a love letter to the baby, tie it to a balloon, and set it free. Release the white balloon with a red balloon representing the blood of Jesus. I kissed the letter and watched the two balloons join together and float upward into the sky. They appeared to me like Jesus holding a tiny hand and leading it to heaven.

I am deeply healed, forgiven, and set free from this painful sin because of God and His unconditional love, grace, and mercy. I made a healthy decision to let God begin to change me. My prayers are that I can be that one person to another woman who is alone, scared, and considering an abortion. I pray that God can work through me to her and let her know that abortion is not the answer. We are all children of God. Every child should live in God's loving care. Do not let anyone talk you into a decision that could affect the rest of your life and the purity of your soul. I made a wrong decision when I was living and thinking in fear. My soul suffered tremendously because of this sin. Put your trust in the Lord, and look for guidance and answers from Him. He will lead you to someone whom you can confide in for the right decision to be made.

> The Spirit of the Lord God is upon me, because the Lord has anointed me to bring good tidings to the afflicted; he has sent me to bind up the brokenhearted, to proclaim liberty to the captives, and the opening of the prison to those who are bound; to proclaim the year of the Lord's

favor, and the day of vengeance of our God; to comfort
all who mourn; (Isaiah 61:1-2)

For I will be merciful toward their iniquities, and I will
remember their sins no more. (Hebrews 8:12)

In this world, women are sometimes the ones punished indiscriminately
for sex. Many are often left feeling scorned, embarrassed, or abandoned.
Some women perhaps benefited least from sex and lost the most by it.
Women are often the ones who find sex an artless humdrum if married
and unspoken shame if not. When a woman is unmarried, having dreams,
hobbies, and positive interests help take the focus off the pressure and
temptation to sin through sex. Don't try to gain the whole world and lose
your soul. Trust God's plan, and know that purity is a blessing.

Let marriage be held in honor among all, and let the
marriage bed be undefiled; for God will judge the immoral
and adulterous. (Hebrews 13:4)

God has shown me a revelation since my baptism, a new life for me
when I came up and out of the waters with the Holy Spirit! The time to
forgive myself for the sins committed in my youth before marriage as I was
a faithful wife in my former marriage. The sins of promiscuity, lust, and
abortion occurred during my life in darkness and despair. I cannot rush
it. It all comes in God's time. I am not defeated. I no longer have to walk
around broken, sad, in pain, shame, weak, discouraged, or depressed. God
is my great healer. I look to Jesus for love. I must speak with my mouth
loudly against Satan trying to rule my mind. I do not have an agreement
with Satan anymore. My mind is the battlefield, but my Savior Jesus is the
winning defeater. Jesus has conquered the grave. I must speak out loudly
about what I want, who I am, and all truth from God. Not ever turning
to sex for love ever again. I believe in marriage, and pray that in God's
timing, a faithful, good man will be brought into my life for commitment.
Until then, I have willingly chosen celibacy. I choose to live with purity
and Jesus.

GOD CHANGES ME

It is important to reflect on who we were before we came to Christ and who we are now in Him to understand and know the love of God. The reality and truth of being saved by the blood of Jesus. The living testaments of the gospel and God's merciful and powerful grace. Understanding and sharing our own personal testimonies with others also have great importance.

Don't ever think that writing in a journal and dating the notes has no meaning. God's intercession is all beautiful timing. Over the years I have jotted notes in a journal, dated it, and set it aside. Particular events happened and I dated those. Then some months, even years later I may review the journal and surprisingly notice similarities. For example, on a particular date a couple years earlier, I wrote about my desires to mentor women who have suffered the same tragedies I have. I took detailed notes about what I wanted to do for them—like pray with them, encourage them, and listen to their stories. On that exact calendar date two years later, I found myself starting my own counseling sessions. Another example, notes taken and read where I helped with a self-defense seminar for women. On that exact day eighteen years later, I was baptized! Seeds that we sow; all that we say, what we do, how we live, and who we influence. Examples we show and choices we make. Words, actions, and thoughts are all seeds to sow.

I journaled notes at a women's retreat I attended one weekend a few years back. The notes state, "I am going to finish writing my book! I believe God calls me to be a writer and help mentor women."

My hope is that others see this through my shared life testimony, through my book as I decide to consider publishing. When we stay silent or self-absorbed, with eyes on ourselves only, we miss the beauty of not healing for ourselves. But more important, we miss God blessing someone else through us. God wants to work through us, not just to us. I pray through my past experiences I can now give women hope, compassion, understanding, insight, and prayers from the heart of God. This is empathy in action. Suffering brings us closer to God. Through my suffering I lived, survived, and received strength only because of God.

One important lesson I have learned and often share with others is that time does *not* heal all wounds. Only Jesus Christ, the Holy Spirit, our heavenly Father can heal us. Until I completely surrendered my heart, pain, and life to God, my soul would never heal from the past. I needed to be spiritually healed. All the dances in life I did and continue to dance to I choose with my eternal partner, Jesus Christ.

As women, sometimes one or more of the painful situations I shared may occur in our lives. My prayer is they never be left unspoken and without compassion and guidance. This following scripture would be a prayer I have for all women. As everything I have now shared, and as I myself have repented, been forgiven, and prayed for righteousness to God, may you all be blessed of the same.

> I appeal to you therefore, brethren, by the mercies of God, to present your bodies as a living sacrifice, holy and acceptable to God, which is your spiritual worship. Do not be conformed to this world but be transformed by the renewal of your mind, that you may prove what is the will of God, what is good and acceptable and perfect. (Romans 12:1–2)

When I turned fifty, I had thankfully come to the seasons of peace, trust, and acceptance.

MY PURPOSE WITH GOD

God gave me a clear perspective about my life story through writing this book. I spent many years in my youth living for me in a survival mode, and then the middle part getting healed and restored. I felt lost and confused with all the pain and suffering that went on for years. Now with Jesus, the truth, the way, the light, I can live the last part of my life seeing other people come alive in their walks with Him.

I began to share my personal testimony from one-on-one trusted individuals to small groups of women at Bible studies, and then to larger groups of church congregations. The first large sharing was the day I was baptized. I had distinct mental arguments with God about this in the hours before the service. God wanted me to verbally testify the rape experience and my claim how He saved me. I didn't want to reveal this personal drama, "No, God, I'm not ready." But then God told me something of great change for me, He said, "It is not about you. Someone in this gathering needs to hear this." God was right. As always. After I bravely shared my dramatic testimony and gave God all the glory, several women came up to me and expressed their need to hear it because of similar experiences. Since that sharing, I didn't want to be selfish anymore and keep quiet about all God's wondrous works and loving changes He brought upon my life. I wanted to share more to influence, inspire, and encourage others to really know and have a loving relationship with our heavenly Father. My prayers are for someone else to accept Christ as their Savior too. Surrender everything and dance with the Lord.

> Do not neglect to do good and to share what you have,
> for such sacrifices are pleasing to God. (Hebrews 13:16)

Studying the Bible and sharing insights with others are very satisfying for me. I can motivate others to know God by the living testimony of my life and openly, confidently telling what He has done for me. I enjoy bringing hope and joy to people living in difficult circumstances. I choose to love, know, and share God more and more each day. The truth is it's not about me; it's about God working in and through me, and making good choices to honor and glorify Him.

Now I would rather have people come to me for the love of hearing my testimony of healing than anything else. I want to help those who suffer for the sake of truth. Help them understand that in the gentleness of Jesus there is power, in His grace there is strength, and in forgiveness there is life. Find strength in Jesus in our weaknesses. See His glory in what is despised. Feel His presence when you are in despair.

I was often told by others that I have some helpful insights to share from my life experiences. God has certainly helped me through these experiences and healed me through each one. Times were indeed rough over the years, but I believe there was a definite purpose in everything I went through. God is doing things in me that I hope will be valuable to many others as I continue to share my heartfelt insight.

Your heart is the core of who you are. Receive God in your heart. Spend time with Him in prayer and meditate on His Word, the Bible. This will help guard your heart as God says to do. Open your heart to encouragement, gratitude, generosity, and a love for Jesus and others. God's hand of favor and love will come upon your life. I have always been grateful for life ever since surviving, living after the rape. I always believed life could be good even though there were hard, tragic days to overcome. The hard days didn't take away my appreciation for life. I always knew God loved me and would help me through those hard days.

Humble yourselves and pray. Speak out God's Word. Let God be glorified by how His grace and love heal all pain and tears. All those years when I was pouring out my heart to God, He was pouring out His grace. God is the light through all darkness. He has a love for each of us. Don't put limits on His abundant power. Share His love every chance you can with your words and actions. Love life, love God.

I am so very grateful to God for everything He has done for me and my son. The most important relationships in my life are with God and my son. I am grateful my son has a relationship with God and decided to be baptized in his teen years. Our salvation and love for Jesus Christ is a beautiful testimony to share with others.

The hardest person to share my testimony with was my son. My pastor at the time said it would be good to let my son know some things about my past. He was a teenager and entering high school the coming year. Prior to approaching the dating scene, I wanted him to understand and respect girls. My son was maturing in both Christianity and age, and just to have that freedom of silence really broken would be important. And, of course, I would never want him to hear my story from someone else first. It was a very hard discussion for me as a mother because all I wanted to do was protect him from the ugly side of life. I wanted to avoid him ever knowing about those dark years in my past. But I trusted God and He was in our house very strongly the evening I told my son. God gave me the strength and the right words to say to him. After sharing, my son openly said the most powerful, beautiful prayer I had ever heard in my life! God was indeed upon the heart of this young man. Hearing his first few praying words, I began to really purge and cry deeply, like I had never done before. Jesus loved us both very strongly that evening. My son's words were so good and powerful. He accepted this sensitive matter very maturely, and I do not regret telling him. The next day I looked at him with a new perspective and saw us drawn closer in a different way. I saw a young man growing in God's favor and us being able to openly communicate as a family in new, mature ways. I still have the responsibility of protecting him, guiding him, and being a mother. But I don't have to shield or overprotect him because I know that God is with him.

My parents overprotected me and always kept silence and avoidance on so many topics in life. I had to grow up pretty fast with hard realities once off that sheltered childhood farm and into the traumas I experienced in my youth. As a parent now I understand protecting our children. But we can't avoid educating our children in all areas of life's lessons, good and evil, that may or may not happen. Our beliefs and relationships with God should begin at home. When we let schools and society teach our children some of the hard facts of life, that is when the pain and problems really begin. Sometime during that year before sharing my story with my son, I remember him asking me about the subject of rape. I don't know if he saw something in a movie he watched, heard it at the school, or why this topic had come up. But I do remember my familiar feelings when he said the word "rape" and how I originally didn't really want to deal with it. Silence and avoidance were on this parent's mind as well. But I didn't want this for my son, and I didn't want to hold back any important life lesson that he might learn from my experiences. I didn't want him learning about the crime of rape and what it really does to a woman from society's perspective. So when the pastor suggested opening up to my son, I knew it was the right thing to do, difficult or not. My son now has compassion concerning the damage caused by mistreating women because his mom went through it. He can use that compassion and treat his future girlfriends and wife with respect and love. Influence his male friends to act accordingly with women as well. An important lesson in life has been shared here with him. More important, he can do God's will and love for the good of whom all he meets.

Forgive others, forgive yourselves. Enjoy the peace only God can give. Celebrate life! Dance a joyous dance in that celebration!

> *J*ournaling: A brief record or diary of daily happenings, writing of general or popular interest.
> *E*mpathy: The understanding and sharing of the emotions and experiences of another person.
> *S*incerely: Honestly, straightforward, genuine.
> *U*ltimately: Relating to or being the most important.
> *S*trengthened: To make, grow, or become stronger or more powerful.

Jesus is the ultimate reason why I am saved, strengthened, and free, sincerely. Because of Him I share my journals of my testimony with great empathy.

> *G*uidance
> *O*n
> *D*ifficulties

My faith in God and His grace are why I am healed and guided away from the difficulties.

> Draw near to God and he will draw near to you. Cleanse your hands, you sinners, and purify your hearts, you men of double mind. Be wretched and mourn and weep. Let your laughter be turned to mourning and your joy to dejection. Humble yourselves before the Lord and he will exalt you. (James 4:8–10)

VISIONS FROM GOD

Visions from God sometimes appeared to me during prayer. One Sunday morning during communion at church, listening to worship music, eyes closed, and my head bowed in prayer, a vision happened. I am giving thanks to the Lord with a heart full of joy, feeling the presence of the Holy Spirit, and just loving God. He showed me an image. He showed me as a little girl running through a field of grass and flowers, laughing, smiling, joyfully giggling as I ran to Him, my Father in heaven. I was wearing a dress, like a cotton jumper style. I thought my age to be around six to eight. This image I could have viewed longer, but I opened my eyes to partake in the communion tray near me.

That night at bedtime, I thought of the special comforting image again and asked God to show it to me more please. I have a small memory of it. But I also feel God was telling me something. Before I became devoted to Christ through baptism, I spent many years running away from things, people, memories. Ran from fear, pain, commitments, everything. I feel deep down inside my heart that since my knowledge and truth of the light in Jesus has been revealed, I want more of Him. I want more of God, more of the Holy Spirit. I am now running to and seeking Him. My youthfulness, born again, renewed childlike faith. God showed me He has me as His child. My childlike faith is being revealed more clearly through the vision. I can run to Him and give Him all my cares. I can love, laugh, and be a free-spirited child knowing God is always there. Run to my Daddy's loving arms. No more running from but just running to God's big heart in childlike faith.

Sometime years later, I had a brief vision of Jesus being dragged with the cross, and I was clinging on. I had my arms wrapped around his legs and was a faint, almost invisible image on that trail to His crucifixion.

At four o'clock one early December morning, I had a spiritual visitor—my mom! I was praying because I couldn't fall back to sleep after I woke up so early. I just found myself saying, "Mom, I love you. I miss you!" All of a sudden, I saw her face as clear as if right there in the room with me. I said, "Oh, Mom, hold me." Then I felt her presence so strong; I felt her hold me. I began crying, overwhelmingly crying, surrendering my love and heart to her. Telling her I missed her, needed her, needed her comfort. I needed to be held. My mom came to me! This experience was so incredibly surreal. Then after a long time crying, I asked the Holy Spirit to bring me joy. I instantly realized the word I said and started giggling. "Joy!" Mama Joy! The word brought so much meaning as being a mother.

ADVERSITIES IN LIFE

God guided both my son and I through many adversities in our lives, but seasons of joy and celebrations came along with them. Where the Spirit of the Lord is there is joy, love, strength, and understanding. During my son's spiritual and physical growth, especially in the teenage years, it was vital for me to be attentive and supportive. As always being the only parent in his life, I am thankful and very proud of how he has grown into a caring, responsible, interesting, fine young man. A young man who has accomplished a missionary trip out of the country at age sixteen, a high school degree, Eagle Scout rank from the Boy Scouts of America, and employment opportunities with high recognition. My son is my greatest accomplishment.

Moving my son and I to a different state for a fresh start after the divorce and losing everything was stressful but mostly a welcomed adventurous change. Stress over the years as a single mother and the head of household, with a low income and at times no income, sometimes overwhelmed my responsibilities. While attending college my first semester, I distinctly remember being at the campus library and needing to print a class assignment I had just typed. I had no money at all, not even the dime needed for the printer. I walked around the library looking at the floors in hope of finding lost change. There it was! I saw a dime! I snatched it up quickly and am reminded again of the hope of God providing as always.

My college degree was earned at the age of forty-three. I worked in the outdoors for several years before, during, and after college. Then an injury from falling while on the job reveals hidden problems in a series of X-rays. I was diagnosed with several spinal conditions that put physical limitations on work and lifestyle. The pain endured through the years was persuasive enough for me to follow my physician's advice to make changes as most of the conditions couldn't be resolved in surgery. So I left my college-earned profession behind and proceeded to seek work that was gentle on my spinal condition and prevented further damage. I continued to photograph professionally for about thirty years. Photography had always been a side income, and I enjoyed having the occasional print published in a few magazines.

For a full year after my son graduated from high school, I struggled with finding work after being laid off from another job. Being selective on types of jobs due to my spinal restrictions and as a woman over age fifty, a little statistics with that in general, were resulting in frustrating rejections. Besides job hunting, I was also house hunting that full year. We had lived at the same rental home for several years, until my son graduated. Then he moved out with a friend, and thus began the empty nest. I temporarily rented a friend's home while trying to buy a house through special low-income programs. It was a long process that was not turning out well, so I continued looking for a permanent rental instead. Another complicated situation with the housing market in my county of residence. I came to a breaking point one day where I cried out to God, "I have no work, no home, and an empty nest. Lord, I am very uncomfortable!" God did bring work, an apartment for one, and a new kind of relationship with my son. All in His own timing.

Music continues to be important in my life. My voice to sing came back, and for a while, I sang in church worship bands, praising the Lord and opening my heart and worship to Him. Dancing continued, just as life continues. Therapeutic dancing in water became an interest to help manage my painful spinal diagnosis. Later a professional opportunity as I trained and became a certified water aerobic instructor. I choreograph my own music and routine to create water aerobic classes with rhythm dancing. This bittersweet dance of life we all live in opens the floor to challenges and celebrations. I choose to choreograph my own rhythm in life that tells my story.

My post-traumatic stress disorder found comfort in both dance therapy and water aerobics. I also received therapy through an eye movement desensitization reprocessing (EMDR) program. During the months of therapy, I experienced beautiful visions. My time in prayer and deep mediation with the Lord during those months was incredible. God revealed Himself to me through these visions. There would be a series of them throughout my time there, each lasting several minutes. Even though I journaled the details of the experience, I hesitate to share them in my writing of this book. The visions are a personal gift, a private time with my Creator, and God meant the healing power of the moments to be for me. I honor and hold these visions as a divine anointing from God. But what I will say is that my fear of knives since the rape is now gone. The detailed visions revealed holding them, trusting God's ways, and releasing the fear and anxiety to Him.

I eventually opened another dream business. A coffee shop with a large dance floor instead of a bakery. My love for hospitality, making espresso, music, dancing, and connecting friends were all enjoyed at this business. There were many evenings I enjoyed my own personal dance floor, turned the music up loud, and released everything that was happening. When I was a teenager, I sang, danced, and wrote songs and poems in my bedroom. The rape and post-traumatic stress disorder struck me down into silence, nonmovement. Now as a woman who has overcome so much, and with my own dance floor, all that music was released within me. The dancing became so awesome and creative.

> Dancing to me is all about loud, passionate music,
> Releasing the emotions to the rhythm.
> It's all about focus.
> Focus on the song, the rhythm, the feeling.
> Your mood, your motion, your experience.
>
> It is learning to do the dance of life alone.
>
> You are alone! You are single! So what?
>
> Dance, dance, dance.
>
> Dance to the dance of life alone.
>
> It's about getting into the song,

The song—not your feelings, not your emotions, not your ability.

Listen to the rhythm, the beat of the song.

Feel it, groove to it, do it.

Dance like you're intoxicated, but you're not.

Uncover, discover, and discard everything that's holding you back.

Dancing helps you feel the rhythm, the rhythm of life.

Feel the music and body movements.

Explore feelings, release energy that's positive or negative.

Develop connectedness between the body and the mind.

Dance, dance, dance.

Dancing to me is all about passion, the music.

The business unfortunately endured severe financial strain, very little community support, and eventually a break-in to force a decision to close. Feelings of disappointment and discouragement consumed me. Amid that, I experienced six months being homeless and sleeping on couches at the business and my son's home. My finances were tied up in business commitments, and no housing was available in a complicated county. The break-in at the business triggered my post-traumatic stress disorder symptoms to very uncomfortable levels. My physical health began to suffer from long-term stress. My son was also experiencing health challenges. In one year he almost drowned in a river while fly-fishing, damaged his shoulder in a recreational bike accident, had a concussion from rolling his pickup in a highway accident, and almost died from a torn esophagus and gastroenteritis attack.

I had reached another breaking point and cried out to God, "I am broken." Concerns as a mother were different now than when raising a young child alone. I had no money, was heartbroken by ending another business dream I worked so hard for, and dreading the job and home searching again. I was tired of living out of suitcases and storage, and exhausted from the lack of sleep on couches, all the decisions to make, coping with fear back in my life, and uncertain what steps to take now as I started over in life again. I struggled with anger and frustration. Nothing made sense. I couldn't understand why every effort I made for a house and an income were not working out. Opportunities created from my dreams I expected to flow smoothly. Instead, they vanished among the crashing rocks in life. I was not liking the rough currents of this river.

But as my faith remained, I finally realized something. It didn't matter what was happening, or did or didn't happen with my dreams and life plans. God is in control and at work in my life. As a believer, I trust Him.

A man's mind plans his way, but the Lord directs his steps. (Proverbs 16:9)

God directed my steps! Used my circumstances to change me! I wanted to let go of the striving, excess hard work, the struggles, the stress, and just dance.

One day you think you've got it all figured out and then things change. The river flows differently. God changes the directional flow of your life. Times when dreams are on hold, and times when they come true. God is always there. Times when you make sacrifices, and other times when you are overwhelmed by the many blessings. But God is always there. God has other plans for me.

God tells us in His Word, the Bible, we can have health in every area of our lives.

Relationships

A new commandment I give to you, that you love one another; even as I have loved you, that you also love one another. (John 13:34)

Mind

for God did not give us a spirit of timidity but a spirit of power and love and self-control. (2 Timothy 1:7)

Body

But he was wounded for our transgressions, he was bruised for our iniquities; upon him was the chastisement that made us whole, and with his stripes we are healed. (Isaiah 53:5)

Soul

Beloved, I pray that all may go well with you and that you may be in health; I know that it is well with your soul. (3 John 1:2)

CIRCLE OF LIFE

My past is defined as grace and healing that the Holy Spirit revealed to me. My present is full of God's gifts. My future is based on the promises of God, all in His perfect timing.

When I moved after my college graduation, I left the small town and a lot of sadness behind. This Montana town rested at the edge of a beautiful lake surrounded by mountains. The college experience gave me a good outlook on life, but I had to work through the grieving process of my mom's death, my son's loss of a father, and all the constant struggles I experienced nonstop in the years since my youth.

Now fifteen years later, an opportunity arose with work and better living conditions that had me deciding to move back to my college town area. I was leaving behind again many grievances from the previous three years of instability.

Too often we think it is something we are meant to do. But really, it's what we are meant to be within God's presence.

God redirects my path of life as I absorb His presence more, one day at a time. Settling in yet another fresh start in my life. Slowing myself down and rediscovering what's really important in life. I am thankful for a new cozy apartment and increasing my water aerobics classes. The beautiful lake near my home I leisurely walk around, surrounded by gorgeous mountain views, and the waters welcome my kayak. In the evenings I listen to music outside and dance on my wood deck. The stars above shine comfort of knowing where God wants me to be and where I am content to stay. Calming waters of a lake feel like home. Peacefulness awaits with the still waters of a lake.

As I reflect on these words, I now realize that I am no longer the river, rough currents and searching. Instead, I have become the lake of contentment.

The circle of life God put me in and revisiting familiarity are all very interesting to me. My son was only in kindergarten when we lived here. I smile at the revisited memories of him as a little boy, climbing in an apple tree and sliding down metal slippery slides in the school playground I now drive by again. I feel revisiting motherhood within myself and memories of my mom's love now bring contentment.

Nature is nurturing me once again as I take the time to plant flowers, ride a bike, kayak and boat the lakes, take leisurely walks, fly a kite, and explore scenic backroads once driven. A close friend I knew when I lived in Colorado surprisingly contacts me. She and I had lost touch over twenty-five years ago. We were friends during my time spent on the typewriter with this book in my small cabin. That our friendship reconnecting during this time when I am determined to complete the book is all very surreal. All very much God's timing.

I am content and thankful that some of the busyness of my life experiences are behind me. I am appreciating a simple life, so I have time to spend with God, my grown son, and my health. I spend more time in prayer and reading devotionals. Allowing God to heal me mind, body, and soul. The visions during these months are reassuring from God. "Oh, what a beautiful safe place!" In prayer one morning, praising Jesus, a beautiful vision comes to me. God appears. His arms wide, reaching down for me. He places His hands under my arms and lifts me up. I am limp, relaxed, welcoming, and float upward. He cradles me, holds me, very lovingly felt. Then comes a breathtaking moment. He gently places me, my whole being, inside Him, inside His heart, deep in the center within Him. This place, oh this place, is so very soft, safe, loving, beautiful, happy, floating, comforting like I have never felt before. I don't want to leave, not ever. God's promises are true! "Oh, what a beautiful safe place!"

Life is sometimes joyful and hopeful, and other times painful and uncertain. But God is there. He is there when you have dreams that come true and there when they end for whatever circumstances. God is there when you're lonely and when you're blessed with loved ones. God loves me and is well pleased with me. When I am weak, He is strong. When I am strong, it's because He is within me, giving me strength. God restores all things. The ultimate reason why I am healed, restored, and strengthened is sincerely because of my Father God. And because of Him, I share my testimony with great empathy.

I made a new friend who doesn't know anything about my past. She expressed how she wants to see me rise above whatever life gave me in hopes it will be a glory story. I believe my life is God's story, and I hope to reveal that every time I share it or write about it. I give God all the glory.

> And after you have suffered a little while, the God of all grace, who has called you to his eternal glory in Christ, will himself restore, establish, and strengthen you. (1 Peter 5:10)

> Peace I leave with you; my peace I give to you; not as the world gives do I give to you. Let not your hearts be troubled, neither let them be afraid. (John 14:27)

FAITH

Rain had come down quite gently that night.
Moisture under my eyes came streaming out,
Understanding the empty words in sight.
Breathe and exhale without any doubt.

All those years trying to be strong.
Something deeper inside of me
Hoping the silent thoughts are all gone,
Understanding empty, solemn empty.

Journals of a past before
Clouds formed as in stillness order.
Through faith, opened to restore
Where quiet and light are absorbed.

You are safe in Jesus's arms, safe.
He carries you, always carries you.
Relax and let the waters flow,
Washing me, calming me.
For by grace you have been saved; you've been saved
Through faith, that beautiful faith.
This is not by your own doing.
It is the gift of God,
Gift of God.
Not because of works; no one should boast.
You've been saved
By God alone.

FINAL THOUGHTS

I started this book from journal notes written one summer at an isolated cabin in Alaska. It was completed in 2020, during quarantine caused by the COVID-19 pandemic. It was an over thirty-year process as each year, each situation added chapters to write about. During the quarantine, I came to believe that God was protecting me again as I had contemplated reopening another coffee shop just months prior.

As I questioned myself about the years of expansion completing this book, a good friend from college shared her insight with me on this. "Well the truth of that matter is you can't write the story until it is complete. Meaning, you had to revisit things and learn new lessons and insights along the way before you could share that knowledge in your book. Had you published a decade or two ago, it would have been premature."

I acknowledge this friend, Grace, for her encouragement, educated editing perspectives, and uplifting prayers when I was completing my book.

I submitted a completed manuscript to a publisher on the day my mother had passed away fifteen years prior. I honor my mother's memories with peace, love, and Joy.

My father passed away shortly before the publishing process of my book was completed. He came to know and love Jesus and is now resting in peace.

I bought a classic boat to cruise on the lake the summer while this book was being published. A little restoration project as the boat is the same year as my birth year.

DISCOVER YOUR OPPOSITES WORKSHEET

Journal your thoughts after each question. This creative mental exercise will help you cope with post-traumatic stress disorder.

Post—Opposite of before

1. Who were you before the trauma: your characteristics, personality, and the way others saw you?

2. What did you like to do before: your hobbies, interests, and enjoyable activities?

3. Where did you enjoy going for fun or relaxation before? What places were important to you?

4. When were your best moments, memories, activities before? What time of the day or what season motivated you the most?

5. Why did you stop?

Traumatic—Opposite of calming

1. Who helps you to remain calm? Think of at least one person you could talk to, trust, and confide in.

2. What helps you to feel calm? What activities and hobbies do you do?

3. Where do you like to go that you find calming?

4. What time of the day do you feel most calm?

5. Why do you not purposely seek calmness?

Stress—Opposite of is relaxation

1. Who helps you relax?

2. What activities help you relax?

3. Where do you like to go to relax?

4. When is the best time of day or week to find time to relax?

5. Why don't you make time to relax?

Disorder—Opposite of order

1. Who helps keep you and your emotions in order?

2. What does it take to keep you and your life in order? Prioritize important things learned to gain order.

3. Where do you like to or can go to feel like you and your life are in order? Perhaps control of your own life is order as well.

4. When do you feel like your life is in order? What is different during those moments?

5. Why do you expect or want order?

ACRONYM

Your Negative to Positive Outlook

Read your answers from the previous worksheet and apply the letter representing the outcome.

Example: P_____/from before; I knew poetry from my youth was important. Therefore, replace the negative effect of post with the positive outlook of writing poetry.

P_____/from your before

T _____/from your calming

S _____/from your relaxation

D _____/from your order

Printed in the United States
By Bookmasters